DATE DUE

APR – 9 1998		
JUL 2 1 1998		
AUG 2 0 1998		
JUL 2 3 1999		
AUG 2 6 1999		
JUL 1 7 2000		
AUG 8 2000		

Demco, Inc. 38-293

ABOUT THE BANK STREET READY-TO-READ SERIES

More than seventy-five years of educational research, innovative teaching, and quality publishing have earned The Bank Street College of Education its reputation as America's most trusted name in early childhood education.

Because no two children are exactly alike in their development, the Bank Street Ready-to-Read series is written on three levels to accommodate the individual stages of reading readiness of children ages three through eight.

○ *Level 1:* GETTING READY TO READ **(Pre-K–Grade 1)**
Level 1 books are perfect for reading aloud with children who are getting ready to read or just starting to read words or phrases. These books feature large type, repetition, and simple sentences.

○ *Level 2:* READING TOGETHER **(Grades 1–3)**
These books have slightly smaller type and longer sentences. They are ideal for children beginning to read by themselves who may need help.

○ *Level 3:* I CAN READ IT MYSELF **(Grades 2–3)**
These stories are just right for children who can read independently. They offer more complex and challenging stories and sentences.

All three levels of The Bank Street Ready-to-Read books make it easy to select the books most appropriate for your child's development and enable him or her to grow with the series step by step. The levels purposely overlap to reinforce skills and further encourage reading.

We feel that making reading fun is the single most important thing anyone can do to help children become good readers. We hope you will become part of Bank Street's long tradition of learning through sharing.

The Bank Street College of Education

For Akiko Takano
— W.H.H.

For my father, Kazuo Otani
— J.O.

For a free color catalog describing Gareth Stevens' list of high-quality books and multimedia programs, call 1-800-542-2595 (USA) or 1-800-461-9120 (Canada). Gareth Stevens Publishing's Fax: (414) 225-0377.
See our catalog, too, on the World Wide Web: http://gsinc.com

Library of Congress Cataloging-in-Publication Data

Hooks, William H.
  Peach Boy / by William H. Hooks ; illustrations by June Otani.
    p. cm. -- (Bank Street ready-to-read)
    Summary: Found floating on the river inside a peach by an old couple, Momotaro grows up and fights the terrible demons that have terrorized the village for years.
    ISBN 0-8368-1662-5 (lib. bdg.)
    [1. Folklore--Japan.] I. Otani, June, ill. II. Title. III. Series.
  PZ8.1.H8525Pe 1996
  398.2'0952--dc20
  [E]   96-1214

This edition first published in 1996 by
Gareth Stevens Publishing
1555 North RiverCenter Drive, Suite 201
Milwaukee, Wisconsin 53212 USA

© 1992 by Byron Preiss Visual Publications, Inc. Text © 1992 by Bank Street College of Education. Illustrations © 1992 by June Otani and Byron Preiss Visual Publications, Inc.

Published by arrangement with Bantam Doubleday Dell Books for Young Readers, a division of Bantam Doubleday Dell Publishing Group, Inc., New York, New York. All rights reserved.

BANK STREET READY TO READ™ is a trademark of Bantam Doubleday Dell Books For Young Readers, a division of Bantam Doubleday Dell Publishing Group, Inc.

Printed in Mexico

1 2 3 4 5 6 7 8 9 99 98 97 96

Bank Street Ready-to-Read™

Peach Boy

by William H. Hooks
Illustrated by June Otani

A Byron Preiss Book

Gareth Stevens Publishing
MILWAUKEE

4

A long time ago
in the land of Japan
there lived an old couple.
They were very poor,
but they did not wish
for gold or fine clothes.
They only wished for one thing.
They longed for a child.

5

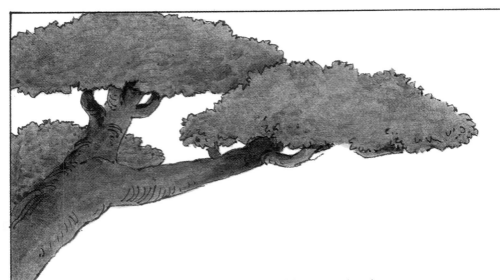

"We are getting old," said the man.
"Soon I will not be able to work.
Who will look after us?
Who will protect us
from the wicked *oni* monsters?"

"I wish we had a son!"
said the woman.
"Wishes can't take care of us,"
said the old man sadly.
Then off he went to cut wood.

The old woman went to the river
to wash clothes.
She rubbed the clothes
on a rock.
Squish, squish, squish.
With every *squish*
the old woman said,
"I wish, I wish, I wish."
After a while she rested.
She was tired of washing
and wishing.

Suddenly she saw something strange
floating in the river.
It was a huge peach!

The woman picked up the peach
and brought it home.
"Not what I wished for," she said,
"but it is a beautiful peach!"

The old man thought so, too.
"Such a peach," he cried.
"It will last us a week!
Let's cut it open right now!"

The old woman got a knife.
She started to cut the peach.
"Stop!" cried a voice.
"Do not harm me!"
The voice came from inside the peach.

13

The old couple couldn't believe
their ears.
Then the peach split in half.
Out jumped a baby boy!
Now they couldn't believe their eyes.

The baby said,
''I'm a gift from God.
God heard your wishes.
I will be your son.''

The old couple was happy.
At last they had a child!
''We'll call you Momotaro!''
they said.
It was a good name
because Momotaro means Peach Boy.

While Momotaro was growing up,
the *oni* monsters stole
from his village.
Everyone was afraid of them,
but no one was willing to fight them.
Momotaro said, "Someday I will."

When he was fifteen years old,
he spoke with his parents.
"It is time I helped you
and my village," he said.
"I will free our land
of the wicked *oni* monsters
who steal our things
and frighten our people."

20

The old couple was worried
but proud of Momotaro, too.
They agreed he could go.

"Be strong, my son,"
said the old man,
and he gave Momotaro his sword.
"Be careful," said the old woman,
and she gave him a bag of dumplings.
"I'll come back soon,"
Momotaro promised.

Momotaro had not gone far
when he met a hungry dog.
The dog growled.
''Here, have a dumpling,''
said Momotaro.

The dog quickly ate the dumpling
and asked, "Where are you going?"
"To fight the *oni* monsters,"
said Momotaro.
"Then I'll help you," said the dog.

They walked a long way
through the woods.
The dog spotted a monkey
and began to bark.
"Where are you going?"
asked the monkey.
"To fight the *oni* monsters,"
said Momotaro.
"Let me help," said the monkey.
"Come along," said Momotaro.
And he gave the monkey a dumpling.

Momotaro led the way,
followed by the dog
and the monkey.
They walked a long way.
At last they saw the fort
where the *oni* monsters lived.

27

Suddenly a hawk flew over them.
"Where are you going?" he cried.
"To fight the *oni* monsters,"
said Momotaro.
"Let me help," said the hawk.
"Come along," said Momotaro,
and he gave the hawk a dumpling.

29

When they reached the fort,
they saw the huge *oni* monsters
looking down from the walls.

''We've come to fight you,''
shouted Momotaro.
The *oni* monsters laughed.
''A boy, a dog, a monkey,
and a hawk!'' they roared.
''We'll squash you like fleas!''

While they were laughing,
the hawk flew over the walls.
He dived at the monsters' heads.
He clawed and pecked them.
An *oni* tried to hit him,
but the hawk was too fast.

33

The monkey ran to the gate.
She climbed up and opened it,
while the hawk pecked
at the monsters.

34

A huge *oni* grabbed
the monkey.
She tried to get away,
but the *oni* was too strong.

Momotaro and the dog dashed
inside the fort.
The dog bit the *oni*'s leg.
The *oni* let the monkey go.

Another *oni* rushed up.
Momotaro stopped him
with his sword.

"All together,"
Momotaro yelled,
"attack the *oni* monsters!"
The hawk pecked their heads.
The monkey bit their arms.
The dog chewed their legs—
and Momotaro cut them down
with his sword.

The monsters were so frightened,
they gave up and
fell to their knees.
They made a promise to Momotaro.
"We'll never steal again.
We'll never again harm your people."

Then they gave Momotaro
all of their stolen treasure.
Momotaro and his friends
loaded the treasure in a cart.

They carried it back
to the old couple's house.

The old couple was overjoyed
to see their son.
"The *oni* monsters will do
no more harm," said Momotaro.
"And this treasure is all for you."

"It's far more than we need,"
said the old man.
"We will share it
with all of our friends,"
said the old woman.

The old couple and Momotaro
lived together happily.
They were never lonely—
not with the dog,
and the monkey,
and the hawk
to keep them company.

AUTHOR'S NOTE

Peach Boy is one of the all-time favorite folktales of Japanese children. It has elements of magic, dreaded ogres, and a trio of engaging animals who help the young hero overcome great odds to bring honor and wealth to his poor family. This retelling offers English-speaking children a chance to enjoy a Japanese classic.

The *oni* (pronounced oh-nee) is a stock character who appears in many Japanese folk and fairy tales. *Onis* are always cast as wicked demons and monsters, who must be overcome by the heroes of the stories.